IMAGES
of America

BLESSED
SOLANUS CASEY

Outside the office door at St. Bonaventure Monastery on Detroit's east side in 1935, Fr. Solanus Casey, Order of Friars Minor Capuchin (OFM Cap), poses with two youngsters on that special day when young Catholics make their First Communion. Countless Detroiters passed through these doors to seek counsel from Solanus, who was the porter or receptionist at the Capuchin monastery from 1924 to 1945. He returned in 1956 and remained until his death on July 31, 1957. The Catholic Church has determined prayers to Solanus resulted in a miracle and has honored him with the title "Blessed." Blessed Solanus Casey is now on the path to possible sainthood. (Capuchin Franciscan Province of St. Joseph.)

ON THE COVER: Dedicated to Mary, the mother of Jesus, this grotto has been a fixture in the backyard of St. Bonaventure Monastery for more than a century. Fr. Solanus Casey often stopped here to pray, as he did in this 1956 photograph by Edwin C. Lombardo of the *Detroit News*. (Walter P. Reuther Library, Archives of Labor and Urban Affairs, Wayne State University.)

IMAGES
of America

BLESSED
SOLANUS CASEY

Patricia Montemurri

ARCADIA
PUBLISHING

Published by Arcadia Publishing
Charleston, South Carolina

Printed in the United States of America

Library of Congress Control Number: 2018942806

For all general information, please contact Arcadia Publishing:
Telephone 843-853-2070
Fax 843-853-0044
E-mail sales@arcadiapublishing.com
For customer service and orders:
Toll-Free 1-888-313-2665

Visit us on the Internet at www.arcadiapublishing.com

*In the words of Blessed Solanus Casey, I "thank God ahead
of time," and I am ever thankful for the blessings in my life
of Paul G. Diehl and our daughter, Natalie J.M. Diehl.*

CONTENTS

ACKNOWLEDGMENTS

My goal with this book was to showcase the impact of Blessed Solanus Casey's life through photographs that capture the ordinary moments of his ministry and the extraordinary events leading to his possible sainthood in the Catholic Church.

These are just a few of the folks who made it possible. Within minutes of telling my idea to Fr. David Preuss, director of the Solanus Casey Center; its business manager, Angela Morris; and former bookstore manager Lisa Stefoff, they were onboard. Colleen Crane, the now-retired public relations director for the Capuchin Franciscan Province of St. Joseph, gave the project the go-ahead shortly thereafter, and they have been boosters and problem-solvers throughout this process.

Brother Michael Gaffney, OFM Cap, who is the graphic and photographic wizard for the Capuchins, was infinitely patient with me. I so appreciated his good humor, good work, and keen eye. Thank you also to so many other Capuchins who helped me, including Larry Webber, Patrick McSherry, Marty Pable, Mike Bertram, and Tom Nyugen. I also thank Brother Richard Merling, the director of the Father Solanus Guild, and staffers Dennis Till and Mary Smith for their support and patience. Many thanks also to Solanus Casey Center staffers Sally McCuen, Jessica Taylor, and Catalina "Cathy" Figueroa-Garibay; and to Tim Hinkle, public relations director for the Capuchin Franciscan Province of St. Joseph. Thank you to Sister Diann Cousino for digging through the archives of the Sisters, Servants of the Immaculate Heart of Mary congregation in Monroe, Michigan; and also to archivist Jeff Hoffman with the Our Lady of Victory Missionary Sisters in Huntington, Indiana; and Brother Roger Deguire, archivist for the Capuchin Franciscan Province of St. Mary in New York City.

Sr. Anne Herkenrath, Father Solanus' great-niece, has lived up to the word great! At the *Michigan Catholic*, editor Michael Stechschulte answered my frequent requests without complaint. Stechschulte, staff writer Dan Meloy, and the *Michigan Catholic* staff deserve kudos for their comprehensive, beautifully executed coverage. Thank you to my former colleagues at the *Detroit Free Press*, Kathy Kieliszewski and Mary Schroeder, for their assistance and contributions.

Thanks go to photographers Jeff Kowalsky and Diane Weiss and graphic artist Martha Thierry for their contributions of excellence. I also thank Michael P. Hagan and Jim Eddy, who answered my calls for help. Lastly, I am grateful for my Arcadia Publishing promoters: Jeff Ruetsche, in acquisitions, and my diligent, resourceful, and ever-patient editors, Caitrin Cunningham and Sara Miller, for listening to my pitches and concerns.

Unless otherwise noted, all images appear courtesy of the archives of the Capuchin Franciscan Province of St. Joseph.

INTRODUCTION

In the United States, it usually takes a National Football League (NFL) team or superstar musical artist to fill up a sports stadium. But in Detroit on November 18, 2017, some 66,000 fans of a gentle Capuchin friar—one who had been dead for 60 years—converged on the city's NFL stadium for a rare Catholic ceremony that recognized Father Solanus Casey as a miracle worker and bestowed upon him the title of "Blessed."

The crowd size was as large as the average per-game season attendance for the Detroit Lions at Ford Field. Metro Detroiters and pilgrims from across the country and overseas came together to witness the moving ritual of beatification.

In the Roman Catholic Church's roster of saints, there is not a single saint who is an American-born priest. Blessed Solanus Casey could become the first American-born male and priest to be designated a saint. All it will take is another miracle.

To legions of his followers, Solanus Casey has always been a saintly man. Long before his 1957 death in Detroit at the age of 86, Father Solanus was known for his healing touch and kind presence. Many longtime Detroit-area Catholics tell of relatives and loved ones who were consoled—even healed of their maladies and afflictions—after they contacted Father Solanus in his post as doorkeeper in churches in Detroit, New York, and Indiana. The Catholic Church did not recognize all those reports as miracles, but faithful believers have no doubt that God was working through Father Solanus to help them.

It is not unusual for many Detroit-area Catholics to cherish stories about encounters with Father Solanus. Among the relatives of my husband, Paul Diehl, family lore recounts that his maternal aunt Mary Ellen Irving Bellaimey was near death as a toddler from polio. Her father and grandfather owned Detroit Stained Glass Works and personally knew Father Solanus. In the era of twice-a-day mail, a letter was dispatched to the doorkeeper at St. Bonaventure Monastery asking for the friar's prayers. On the same day, a note in Father Solanus' handwriting arrived at Mary Ellen's house in southwest Detroit assuring the family that the child's recovery was at hand.

As a journalist at the *Detroit Free Press*, I wrote about Solanus' appeal and impact. In 1987, it was front-page news when his remains were exhumed from the monastery's backyard cemetery. They were examined for signs of decay, because its absence could indicate holy intervention, part of the process to advance his cause for sainthood. In Rome, I spoke to Capuchins who worked on the rigorous documentation required by the Vatican to evaluate Father Solanus' suitability for beatification and sainthood. And I was thrilled to be asked to return to the *Free Press*, nearly two years after I retired, to cover the Beatification Mass.

In so many ways, the young man born as Bernard Francis "Barney" Casey led the typical life of so many Catholic immigrants from pioneer families who came to America. He was a good athlete, playing baseball and tennis, and was fond of a pool stick and beer with his hot dogs. Barney fell in love, too, and even proposed to a young Wisconsin teenager whose mother then sent her off to boarding school. But he felt a call to the religious life, as did the sons and daughters of many immigrant families. Even when Solanus' book-smarts were questioned by his religious superiors, he was not deterred. When he was ordained a Capuchin, his superiors limited the scope of his priestly duties.

Father Solanus cheerfully carried out what was requested of him and maintained a welcoming demeanor after being ordained a simplex priest, unable to preach on matters of theological doctrine or hear confessions.

"That is the real miracle to me," Fr. David Preuss, OFM Cap, who directs the Solanus Casey Center in Detroit, told the *Michigan Catholic*. "This is a man who should have been bitter. He was a preacher who couldn't preach. A confessor who couldn't hear confessions. He accepted that as God's will, that if I'm going to be the receptionist, I'm going to be the best receptionist there ever was."

Since Solanus Casey was ordained in 1904, the Capuchins have recorded hundreds if not thousands of stories from people who came to visit the friar with their concerns and requests and then reported that wonders or unexplained healings (or "favors," as they came to be called) ensued. There are stories of women who were told they would never have children, yet after a visit to Father Solanus, they were with child. Solanus kept ledgers and notebooks filled with stories of recoveries and cures from cancer and disease after families asked for prayers. The television series *Unsolved Mysteries*, hosted by actor Robert Stack from 1987 to 2002, filmed in Detroit to recreate the story of a local woman who said her breast cancer was healed through the intercession of Father Solanus.

Father Solanus even gets some credit for saving an icon of Detroit's automobile industry. In December 1925, Chevrolet autoworker John McKenna was afraid he would soon be out of a job because of plummeting auto sales. McKenna asked Father Solanus to enroll the company in the Seraphic Mass Association to harness the prayers of Capuchins worldwide for the company's benefit. A few days later, McKenna returned to report he had worked overtime the last two days, and Chevrolet had just received an order for 45,000 cars.

The Catholic Church's saint-makers never recognized any of these wonders as miracles—at least, not until September 2012, when a pilgrim from Panama knelt at Solanus' tomb in Detroit. Paula Medina Zarate, a retired Panamanian schoolteacher, prayed at Solanus' tomb for friends and family. As she rose from the tomb, she sensed a voice telling her to pray for herself, too. She had suffered all her life from a disfiguring genetic skin disease. In the minutes and hours afterward, thick sheets of her diseased skin fell away from her body, revealing a smooth, soft texture underneath. It defied medical explanation, doctors and scientists said. It was a miracle, the Vatican decreed.

The altar used for Solanus' Beatification Mass at Detroit's Ford Field was the same museum-quality piece used for the 1987 visit of Pope John Paul II, now a saint, for the Mass at the now-demolished Pontiac Silverdome in a Detroit suburb.

"The Catholic Church in this country has never seen anything like this," said Rocco Palmo, a Philadelphia-based Vatican observer who authors the Catholic website *Whispers in the Loggia*.

Such crowds have greeted popes but have not gathered to celebrate long-dead Capuchin priests, said Palmo. Solanus' elevation highlights "ordinary people who bring Jesus to the world around them."

On the day after Solanus' beatification, Pope Francis extolled the friar's virtues in his weekly Sunday address to the crowds in St. Peter's Square.

Blessed Solanus Casey was "a humble and faithful disciple of Christ, who distinguished himself with an untiring service to the poor," the pope said. "May his witness help priests, religious and laity to live with joy the link between the announcement of the Gospel and the love for the poor."

One

FAMILY, FAITH, AND A CALLING

Blessed Solanus was born Bernard Francis Casey on November 25, 1870, in Oak Grove, Wisconsin, on the banks of the Mississippi River not far from St. Paul, Minnesota. One of ten boys and six girls born to Irish immigrant parents, he was named after his father, Bernard, and nicknamed Barney. Two of his siblings, Mary Ann and Martha, died in an 1878 diphtheria epidemic, a scourge that also left Barney with a speech impediment. His family posed for this portrait on August 14, 1892, in Superior, Wisconsin, when Solanus was home from seminary studies. Solanus is seated third from left on the porch. Pictured are, from left to right, (first row) John, Margaret, mother Ellen, Genevieve, father Bernard, Grace, and Thomas; (second row) Edward, Leo, Solanus, Jim, Ellen, Patrick, Owen, and Gus. Maurice is holding a guitar at far right. The family lived in several towns in Wisconsin, and the siblings were playmates. On the family baseball team, Barney did not use a glove when he played catcher.

At a c. 1860 Fourth of July picnic in Maine, Irish immigrants Ellen Murphy and Bernard Casey met and fell in love. Ellen, born in County Armagh, was eight when her family arrived in Boston. Later, she worked in textile mills near Portland, Maine. Bernard James Casey was born in County Monaghan and worked as a shoemaker in Boston. They married on October 6, 1863, at St. James Church in Salem, Massachusetts.

In Wisconsin, the Casey family bought 80 acres of land about four miles south of Prescott, Wisconsin, not far from St. Paul, Minnesota. Solanus was baptized on December 18, 1870, at a mission church a few miles away from today's St. Joseph Catholic Parish in Prescott, where Sr. Geralyn Misura established a Father Solanus Guild chapter and here holds a pamphlet depicting the original mission building. (Photograph by Nikki Horihan.)

This wood-carved statue of Father Solanus was commissioned years ago by the late Robert and Jean Bruegl, whose Oak Grove property was the home of the Casey family farm. A young Barney Casey made his First Communion at St. Patrick Church in Hudson, Wisconsin, in 1883. The Casey family also lived near Trimbelle, Wisconsin, and attended church at St. Mary's in Big River. As a teenager, Barney courted and proposed to a young woman from the area, Rebecca Tobin. Her mother blocked a marriage by sending Rebecca off to boarding school. (*West Central Wisconsin Catholic*; photograph by Joyce Uhlir.)

The historic baptismal archives maintained by St. Joseph Catholic Parish in Prescott, Wisconsin, recorded, in Latin, the baptism of Bernard Francis Casey on December 18, 1870. It lists his parents' names as well as those of his godparents, Thomas and Catherine Mannion. (Photograph by Brother Nathan Linton, OFM Cap.)

Barney Casey moved to Stillwater, Minnesota, in the late 1880s. It is where he found work as a logger, hospital orderly, and bricklayer. It is also where his maternal uncle Fr. Maurice Murphy was pastor of St. Michael Parish and where Barney made his confirmation in 1890. The church now features a stained-glass window of Father Solanus. (*West Central Wisconsin Catholic.*)

Barney Casey went to prison—to work as a guard! At the Stillwater State Prison, he befriended notorious outlaws. The Younger brothers, Cole, Jim, and Bob, were incarcerated here after numerous robberies with the infamous Jesse James gang. After a failed robbery at Northfield's First National Bank in 1876, the brothers were sentenced to 25 years at Stillwater. (Washington County Historical Society.)

"The closest the surviving Younger brothers ever got to heaven was a prison guard who may be declared a saint by the Roman Catholic Church." That is what historian Brent Peterson wrote in a 2003 article for *True West* magazine. Barney Casey is remembered as a good-hearted, teenaged prison guard, liked enough that one of the Younger brothers made him a small wooden chest. Even after leaving the job, Barney came back to visit. The photograph at right portrays, clockwise from the top, Cole, Bob, and Jim Younger. Pictured below is a contingent of prison guards during the era of Casey's employment, but it is not established whether he was part of the photograph. (Right, Minnesota Historical Society; below, Washington County Historical Society.)

Barney Casey moved to Superior, Wisconsin, on the shores of Lake Superior and across the state line from Duluth, Minnesota, in about 1890 to work on the new electric streetcar line. His family was also relocating to the area. In autumn 1891, while conducting the streetcar, he witnessed a drunken man stabbing a woman to death on the tracks. "The scene remained with him," wrote biographer James P. Derum. "To him, the brutal stabbing and the sailor's hysterical cursing symbolized the world's sin and hate and man-made misery." (Douglas County Historical Society.)

In 1891, at age 20, Barney entered St. Francis de Sales Seminary in Milwaukee to study for the diocesan priesthood. His studies were in German, the predominant language of the city's many Catholic immigrants. He struggled with some classes and was saddened when his superiors suggested he leave in 1895 and try joining a religious order. (Photograph by Michael P. Hagan.)

Barney Casey prayed for direction. In a dream, he heard the Blessed Mother Mary urging him to "go to Detroit." That is where St. Bonaventure Monastery, built in 1883–1884 and run by the Capuchin Franciscan Order, welcomed him on Christmas Eve 1896. On January 14, 1897, Barney donned the Capuchins' brown habit and sandals. He took a new name from St. Francis Solano, a Spanish missionary priest who ministered to slaves and outcasts in the 1600s in Peru.

Now known as Brother Solanus, Barney Casey studied in Milwaukee at the Capuchin seminary at St. Francis of Assisi Church. A part of the Capuchin friary here dates back to 1869, and the church was built in 1876. (Photograph by Michael P. Hagan.)

As before, Solanus struggled with his coursework. His superiors ordained him on July 24, 1904, as a "sacerdos simplex," a designation which prevented him from hearing confessions or preaching sermons on Catholic doctrine. In this photograph of seminary classmates, Solanus is at center in the second row.

The newly ordained Father Solanus celebrated his first Mass at St. Joseph in Appleton, Wisconsin. It was the Capuchin-run church closest to his parents, who traveled 200 miles from Superior, Wisconsin, to attend. Solanus had not seen his mother in eight years. At St. Francis of Assisi Church in Milwaukee, the center column of this collage depicts the Appleton church and three little girls who attended Solanus' first Mass. Fr. Marty Pable (pictured), OFM Cap, lived with Father Solanus at one time. (Photograph by Michael P. Hagan.)

Father Solanus served three New York City parishes after his ordination. His first assignment was at the Monastery of the Sacred Heart in Yonkers, New York, pictured at right, where he was assigned sacristan duties, such as caring for the vessels and vestments. Later, he was made the parish's porter or doorkeeper, greeting those who were ailing physically and spiritually and sought counseling at the church. He came to be known for eloquent, inspiring talks—dubbed "feverinos" by his fellow friars. Below, friars pose in 1912 with young men in suits considering futures as Capuchins. Father Solanus is standing at center in the third row.

Sacred Heart Church
Yonkers, New York

At Sacred Heart, Father Solanus oversaw the altar boys. In the above photograph, he is at far right in the third row. In the below image, he is pictured second from the right in the front row with his fellow Capuchins. After Solanus' beatification, New York City cardinal Timothy Dolan visited the Monastery of the Sacred Heart to celebrate a Mass in Blessed Solanus' honor. (Both, Capuchin Franciscan Province of St. Mary.)

In October 1913, Father Solanus was able to join his family to celebrate his parents' 50th wedding anniversary. He took a train to Seattle, Washington, where many family members had relocated. "His Capuchin habit and long beard made him, to most of his fellow travelers, an almost sensationally interesting figure; many of them had never before laid eyes on a friar," wrote his biographer James Patrick Derum. The above photograph is of the Casey parents and siblings, including Father Solanus, who is seated at far right next to his mother, Ellen. The below photograph includes in-laws and grandchildren, with Solanus standing third from right in the back row; Solanus' handwriting at the bottom of the picture marks the event.

19

Two other Casey brothers became priests. Maurice Casey, pictured at right, was ordained in 1911 at age 44 for the Diocese of Helena, Montana, and spent several years ministering on the Blackfeet Indian Reservation. Edward Casey, pictured at left, attended St. Paul Seminary in the Archdiocese of St. Paul/Minneapolis and was ordained in 1912. He ministered in Minnesota before working in Australia and later the Philippines. In his own hand, Solanus wrote on the photograph: "All ye servants of the Lord, bless the Lord, Praise and exalt him above all forever."

From 1918 to 1921, Father Solanus was assigned to Our Lady of Sorrows Parish in Manhattan as a doorkeeper and the leader of Young Ladies Sodality. In the above photograph, he is seated second from the right. In the below photograph, he gazes at the church's statue of Mary, the mother of Jesus. From 1921 to 1924, Solanus was at Our Lady Queen of Angels in East Harlem, where he visited prisoners in a nearby jail. His biographer Fr. Michael Crosby, OFM Cap, wrote that Father Solanus came to know its inmates personally and distributed Christmas cards to them.

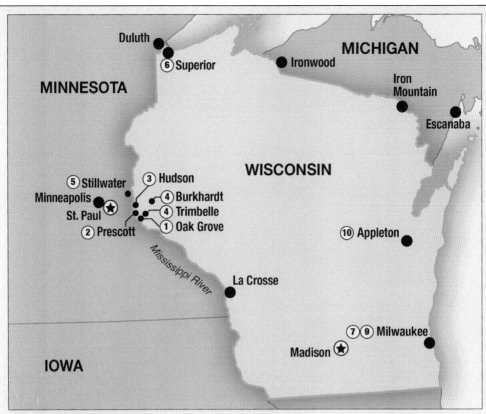

THE LIFE OF BLESSED SOLANUS CASEY

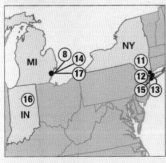

1. Born Nov. 25, 1870 as Bernard Francis Casey Oak Grove, WI.

2. Baptized Dec. 18, 1870 St. Joseph Catholic Church in Prescott, WI.

3. Received First Communion in 1883 at St. Patrick Church, Hudson, WI.

4. Casey family lived in other homes near Trimbelle and Burkhardt, WI. Finished district school in Burkhardt in 1887.

5. Worked in Stillwater, MN, as a lumber logger and prison guard in the late 1880s.

6. Worked in Superior, WI as a streetcar conductor in 1890-91.

7. Enrolled at St. Francis de Sales Seminary in Milwaukee, WI in 1892, but left in 1896 on advice of superiors to withdraw because of grades.

8. Arrived at St. Bonaventure Monastery in Detroit, MI on Christmas Eve, 1896 to enter the Capuchin order. In January 1897, invested as a Capuchin novice and given name of Francis Solanus.

9. Studied at Capuchin monastery at St. Francis of Assisi in Milwaukee. Ordained a Capuchin priest on July 24, 1904.

10. July 31, 1904: Celebrated first mass at St. Joseph Church, Appleton, WI.

11. Aug. 4, 1904 to July 1918: Assigned to Sacred Heart Friary, Yonkers, NY.

12. July 1918 to Oct. 1921: Assigned to Our Lady of Sorrows Parish, New York, NY.

13. Oct. 21, 1921 to Aug. 1924: Assigned to Our Lady Queen of Angels Parish, Harlem, NY.

14. Aug. 1, 1924: Arrived at St. Bonaventure Monastery, Detroit MI and stayed as its doorkeeper until July, 1945.

15. July 23, 1945 to April 25, 1946: Transferred to St. Michael Parish in Brooklyn, NY.

16. April 25, 1946 to Jan. 12, 1956: Semi-retired at St. Felix Friary, Huntington, IN.

17. Returned to St. Bonaventure Monastery in Detroit for medical care. Died at St. John Hospital, Detroit on July 31, 1957.

Map by Martha Thierry

These are the places where Fr. Solanus Casey lived and ministered. Not long after he was ordained in Wisconsin, his home state, most of his family and siblings had moved to the West Coast. His assignments did not bring him back to Wisconsin. Through his ministry, he became a New Yorker, a Hoosier, and a Detroiter. (Graphic by Martha Thierry.)

Two

GOD'S DOORKEEPER IN DETROIT

Father Solanus opened many doors in Detroit when, on August 1, 1924, he was assigned to St. Bonaventure Monastery, the place where he joined the Capuchin Order in 1897. In New York, he had gained a reputation as a wonder-worker and spiritual healer. "Personal problems were being resolved; marriages were achieving peace; people with sicknesses were saying they were healed," wrote biographer Fr. Michael Crosby, OFM Cap, of Solanus' work in New York. Such reports followed Father Solanus' arrival in Detroit. "I have plenty to keep myself busy for at least 18 hours a day," Solanus wrote to one of his sisters from his new post. Here, he is pictured with Father Mathias Nack (right) in 1942 at the entrance to the building next to St. Bonaventure where Solanus cofounded the Capuchin Soup Kitchen during the Great Depression.

23

Father Solanus is entertained by a friendly canine while visiting the farm of Mr. and Mrs. Ed Bishop near Detroit in 1935. The Capuchin Order traces its roots to the ministry of St. Francis of Assisi, who is known for his special affinity with all of God's creatures and is the Catholic Church's patron saint of animals.

Father Solanus (right) stands outside the monastery office door in 1939 with other Capuchins Father Alphonse Heckler (left) and Brother Francis Spruck. The monastery enlarged the office space and waiting area near the door to accommodate the growing number of visitors coming to see Father Solanus.

In June 1929, Father Solanus was part of the celebration when Our Lady of Redemption Melkite Catholic Parish dedicated its new church on McDougall Street near Charlevoix Street in Detroit, about 1.5 miles away from St. Bonaventure Monastery. The parish was founded in 1920 to serve immigrants from Lebanon and the Middle East, and its members are part of one of the Catholic Church's Eastern Rite branches. In 1982, the parish moved to the Detroit suburb of Warren. The Detroit church is still in use by members of a Protestant congregation. The image at right is a cropped close-up of Father Solanus standing in the crowd (pictured above) that spilled out into the intersection. The photograph of the crowd hangs at the Solanus Casey Center in Detroit. In January 2018, a national gathering of young adult Melkite Catholics met in the Detroit area and visited the tomb of Blessed Solanus.

This photograph shows Father Solanus at his desk in Detroit. He had scribbled a reflection about himself—"Poor Sinner"—under his image. He did not always stay at his desk but often went out to visit those too sick to visit him. His driver was often William Tremblay, who also drove the Capuchin across the Ambassador Bridge over the Detroit River into Windsor, Canada, to visit those in need. Biographer Catherine M. Odell recounted in her book that a Capuchin estimated that in 1940 and beyond, as many as 150 to 200 people per day stopped at St. Bonaventure to ask for a blessing from Solanus, especially as more served in the armed forces during World War II.

In July 1883, St. Bonaventure Monastery began on a two-acre plot in an area known as Russell's Grove. It was on the edge of Detroit's city limits at the time and was across the street from the Mount Elliott Catholic Cemetery. Fr. Bonaventure Frey, OFM Cap, a cofounder of the Capuchin Order's presence in the United States, purchased the property for $5,000. The friars moved in during January 1884.

"They are hungry, get them some soup and sandwiches." So said Father Solanus to those at the door during the Great Depression. At first, Solanus would give away part of the monastery's supper provisions, angering the cook. The Capuchin Soup Kitchen's other cofounder, Fr. Herman Buss, OFM Cap, recounted that Solanus said, "Just wait and God will provide," when food ran out once. Solanus asked the men to pray the Our Father. Just then, a bakery man arrived with a basket full of food. "He had this whole truck full of stuff . . . When the men saw this . . . tears were running down their cheeks," Buss said. Above, Father Solanus ladles soup. Below, he is working the tables.

In the above photograph, Father Solanus helps serve meals at the soup kitchen. Below, Solanus helps advertise a soup kitchen fundraiser. Superimposed on the photograph is a shot of Fr. Alphonse Heckler, OFM Cap. Solanus often asked businessmen to donate money. Biographer Michael Crosby wrote that on trips to farms, Solanus "revealed a strength that lay hidden in his scrawny frame" while heaving sacks of vegetables. Solanus also compelled his drivers to recite at least one rosary on the ride.

This illustrates a typical day's work for Father Solanus in Detroit. At his desk, he met with visitors, listened to their concerns, and prayed with them. Father Solanus asked visitors ringing the doorbell to enroll in the Seraphic Mass Association, a 50¢ donation to help the Capuchins with their overseas missions. Soon, his visitors reported that their prayers for favors or good health were answered.

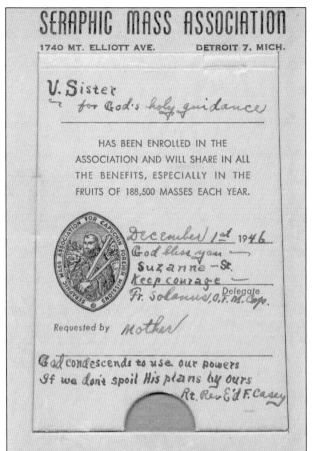

SERAPHIC MASS ASSOCIATION

1740 MT. ELLIOTT AVE.   DETROIT 7, MICH.

V. Sister
for God's holy guidance

HAS BEEN ENROLLED IN THE
ASSOCIATION AND WILL SHARE IN ALL
THE BENEFITS, ESPECIALLY IN THE
FRUITS OF 188,500 MASSES EACH YEAR.

December 1st 1946
God bless you
Suzanne – St.
Keep courage
Fr. Solanus, O.F.M. Cap.   Delegate

Requested by *Mother*

God condescends to use our powers
If we don't spoil His plans by ours
Rt. Rev. Ed F. Casey

Here is the Seraphic Mass Association card for Suzanne Molloy, who became a nun with the Sisters, Servants of the Immaculate Heart of Mary congregation in Monroe, Michigan. Solanus wrote a note quoting his brother, Fr. Edward Casey. The Casey and Molloy families were linked because Suzanne's paternal aunt was married to Father Solanus' brother Leo Casey. Suzanne's brother James, inspired by Solanus, later became a priest. (Sisters, Servants of the Immaculate Heart of Mary Archives.)

Solanus' two brothers who were priests visited with him in Detroit in the 1920s. Pictured here are Maurice (left), Father Solanus (center), and Edward.

In these 1943 photographs, Solanus poses with well-wishers in front of the church door of St. Paul's Catholic Church in Detroit, a parish for immigrants from Malta. The Maltese church was located at Fourth and Plum Streets in the Corktown neighborhood near Detroit's old Tiger Stadium. The church was bulldozed for the Lodge Freeway around 1960. Solanus was fond of a cheesecake made by church member Evelyn Cefai, who was the sister of the church's pastor, Fr. Michael Cefai.

December held great meaning for Father Solanus. He said that he had heard the voice of Mary, the mother of Jesus, on December 8, the day of the Feast of the Immaculate Conception, telling him "go to Detroit" to enter the Capuchin Order. Solanus then traveled to Detroit and arrived on Christmas Eve 1896 to enter the Capuchin life.

Father Solanus loved to play the violin—be it to serenade the Blessed Mother statue in the church or to tap toes to the Irish ditty "Mother Machree." However, he was not known for playing it well, and the other friars often put their fingers in their ears.

In June 1945, Father Solanus traveled to Seattle for his nephew John McCluskey's ordination and then to California. He wanted to visit his brother Fr. Edward Casey, pictured at right, after Edward's release from a Japanese prisoner-of-war camp in the Philippines, where he had ministered. Solanus used a cardboard box for luggage and wore a threadbare habit on the trip. His sister-in-law Martha Casey recalled that other clerics "laughed at his dress and funny little hat, but were very much ashamed when this holy man went on his knees and asked for their blessing. They remarked that they should have been the ones to get on their knees and ask his blessing." The photograph below is a portrait taken in Seattle.

When he returned to Detroit from California, Solanus was reassigned in August 1945 to St. Michael Parish in Brooklyn, New York, pictured below. At left is a portrait he inscribed while living in Brooklyn. The move was supposed to lighten his load, but he wrote to his aide in Detroit, Brother Leo Wollenweber, "that during the 9 or 10 months I was at St. Michael's, it was very seldom, if ever, that I was without letters to acknowledge, even though I sometimes worked on them till after midnight. God be praised." His niece Sr. Bernadine Casey compiled a book of letters written by Solanus.

Three

SHINING IN THE TWILIGHT YEARS

In April 1946, after just nine months in Brooklyn, Father Solanus was assigned to St. Felix Friary in Huntington, Indiana, not far from Fort Wayne. It was designed as retirement, but Solanus was not the retiring type. Many came knocking at his door to see him, including the faithful from Detroit. The friary was built in the Spanish Mission style in 1928 and named after an Italian Capuchin priest from the 1500s who was known to heal the sick. St. Felix Friary was then home to some 60 Capuchins, including young seminarians as well as retirees. In 1980, the Capuchins sold the friary to a Protestant congregation. Philanthropist John Tippman bought the property in 2010 and renovated it; it is now known as St. Felix Catholic Center.

At his desk at St. Felix, Father Solanus sat under a wall-hanging depicting Capuchin missionaries who were canonized saints by the Roman Catholic Church and the world continents where they ministered. The bucolic setting of St. Felix was supposed to insulate Father Solanus from the urgency of life in Detroit. Yet, he was still besieged for help. "Every time the phone rang, it was for him. They'd ask 'Can I speak to Father Solanus?'" said Fr. Marty Pable, OFM Cap, who was a college seminarian at St. Felix during part of Solanus' tenure in Indiana. Pable said mailmen would deliver boxes of letters to Solanus daily. Solanus was often praying in the chapel at 4:00 a.m., well before the 5:15 a.m. scheduled prayer. After lunch, however, it was not unusual to find him playing billiards in a rec room.

In 1947, Father Solanus traveled from Huntington to Detroit for a celebration of his Golden Jubilee to mark 50 years since his first profession as a Capuchin Friar at St. Bonaventure in January 1897. This photograph was taken by Solanus' longtime aide in Detroit, Brother Leo Wollenweber. He was a young friar assigned to help carry, sort, and record the bags of mail that arrived at St. Bonaventure for Father Solanus.

In Detroit, there was a fine celebration awaiting Solanus for his Golden Jubilee. Several siblings traveled to the party in Detroit, which included a Mass. He is pictured above with his sister Grace Brady (left) and brothers Owen Casey (right) and Msgr. Edward Casey. In the below photograph, several nieces and nephews also surround Solanus.

Fr. Simon Hesse, OFM Cap, who was
director of the lay volunteers known
as the Third Order Franciscans in
Detroit, presented Solanus with a
chalice at the jubilee celebration.
Other Capuchins joined Hesse and
Solanus for the below photograph.
The Third Order Franciscans,
referred to today as the Secular
Franciscans, are men and women,
either married or single, who devote
their lives to Franciscan ideals
while living in the secular world.

Father Solanus received well-wishers in a long line at the reception, as shown in the above photograph. When Solanus was seated at the main table, he was flanked by Msgr. Edward Casey, his brother, who flew in from St. Paul, Minnesota. Their sister Grace is reaching out for a handshake with Solanus.

The Detroit newspapers ran a story about Solanus' return to Detroit for his golden jubilee, and thousands clamored to join the celebration. In the below photograph, Solanus addressed the crowd. According to biographer Michael Crosby, Solanus wrote the following for a prayer card to be distributed to the faithful: "Fifty years in the Order, almost unnoticed, have slipped away from me into eternity. Thither I hope to follow before half another fifty, trusting in the merciful goodness of God!"

Father Solanus posed with fellow friars at St. Felix in 1947. From left to right, they are Frs. Herbert Mathieu, Damasus Wickland, Dominick Meyer, Mathias Nack, Solanus Casey, Elmer Stoffel, Michael Reider, and Ambrose DeGroot.

In 1948, Solanus' great-niece Anne Herkenrath traveled from Seattle to visit with Father Solanus. She asked her Uncle Barney about joining the convent. She was with her cousins, Solanus' great-nephews Dean and James Conley from Chicago. "Do I have a vocation or not? Do I go into the convent or not?" she said she asked Solanus. "That's between you and God," she says he told her. She entered the Sisters of the Holy Names of Jesus and Mary, in Seattle. (Sr. Anne Herkenrath.)

At the St. Felix Friary, there were acres of forestland and paths for Father Solanus to stroll. The friars also kept beehives on the property. Fr. Marty Pable, OFM Cap, was in his seminary college years in Huntington during part of Solanus' tenure there. Father Solanus, he said, worked with the bees without any gloves or fear and was never stung. Solanus biographer Fr. Michael Crosby said Solanus was fascinated by the bees' movement, even when they landed on his hand. Solanus would exclaim, "My dear God, how could you have created such a marvelous thing!" Pable said, "He never wore protective clothing. He'd go out there with his bare hands and reach in." Once, Solanus demonstrated to another Capuchin how to identify the queen bee of the hive. "Father, I'm from New York," said the fellow, "I can't tell the queen bee from the Queen Mary!" Casey much enjoyed strolling around the grounds. Fr. Gus Seubert, OFM Cap, recounted how quickly Solanus could respond to a phone call at St. Felix, even when he had to trot in from the fruit orchards out back. The friary's bell system would ring twice when there was a phone call or visitor to see Solanus. "He was in his 80s, but he'd come running," recalled Seubert. Sometimes, Seubert overheard Solanus taking a phone call. "Seldom did you hear him say much. He'd just be listening" and punctuating the calls with "uh-huhs" of acknowledgment and concern.

Father Solanus was known for taking his time with all well-wishers. In the above photograph, he met with the Carrico family at his St. Felix office around 1952. Members of the Carrico family worked at Our Sunday Visitor, the publishing company based in Huntington, Indiana, which has a weekly Catholic newspaper of the same name and has published books and material on Solanus. Pictured at left is the Capuchin priest with another one of the Catholic faithful who visited with him in Indiana.

Well-wishers often brought home-baked goodies. In his book *The Porter of St. Bonaventure*, biographer James Patrick Derum writes, "Women, proud of their culinary skill, brought him such offerings as pies, and these also were found in strange places—shelves behind rows of books being a favorite location." While the friars marveled at Solanus' nature, they also were perplexed by some of his eccentricities. Fr. Benedict Groeschel, who also knew fame as a television personality, resided with Father Solanus at St. Felix. "If he had one eccentricity it was the fact he put all of his food in the same dish at the same time. It could be mashed potatoes and ice cream, but it still went in the same dish," Groeschel recalled in *Solanus Casey: The Official Account of a Virtuous Life* by Michael Crosby, OFM Cap. Groeschel also stated the following: "In the course of my life, I had the opportunity to observe several people who were known for holiness, some of whom are living and some of whom are deceased. These people all had reputations for heroic virtue. Father Solanus was the most extraordinary. I could easily say without any hesitation that he was the greatest human being I have ever known."

James Molloy often visited Father Solanus in Detroit, where Molloy grew up. Molloy's paternal aunt was married to Solanus' brother Leo. Molloy studied for the priesthood and was ordained in Detroit on April 23, 1950. In a note, Solanus wrote that he would be in attendance when Molloy celebrated his first Mass. Father Solanus made good on his promise and is shown above on April 30, 1950, at a Detroit church as Molloy presides at Mass. Molloy served mostly in parishes in the Diocese of Rockford, Illinois. (Both, Patricia Molloy.)

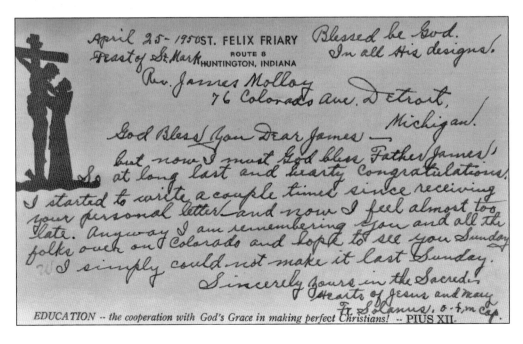

Father Solanus attended the reception following Fr. James Molloy's first celebration of Mass. Molloy is seated to the left of Father Solanus. Molloy's mother, Frances, is seated to the right of Father Solanus.

A congregation of religious sisters lived near the St. Felix Friary in Huntington, Indiana. Father Solanus poses here with Sr. Fidelis Roels, second from right, and Sr. Valeria Foltz, members of the Our Lady of Victory Missionary Sisters. The young lady second from left was a niece of Sister Fidelis. (Our Lady of Victory Missionary Sisters.)

The year 1954 marked 50 years since Father Solanus' ordination as a Capuchin priest at St. Francis of Assisi in Milwaukee. The church at St. Felix Friary was not large enough to accommodate the crowd for the Jubilee Mass. Publicity in the Detroit newspapers about Solanus' milestone brought a surge of crowds from Michigan. They filled the pews at St. Mary's Catholic Church in Huntington on July 28, 1954. In the below photograph, Father Solanus is distributing Communion at the Mass.

The *Detroit Times* updated readers about Father Solanus as he celebrated his 50th anniversary in the priesthood in 1954. The paper noted that the friar, then 83, "stands amazingly erect, although his tall frame is gaunt in its brown homespun habit from many decades of fasting and self-denial. But his most striking characteristics are his eyes . . . the eyes of a man 50 years younger."

This is a classic portrait of Father Solanus. Here, he was smiling and serene, and his eyeglasses had red frames. Solanus was often photographed in a contemplative pose. But his biographer Michael Crosby wrote that Solanus also showed flashes of temper. "To say that in his later years, Solanus Casey never became impatient or angry would not be truthful," wrote Crosby. "Invariably his impatience and anger were goaded in response to deliberate or careless actions by others, as with altar boys who misbehaved during Mass or devotions, people who did not participate regularly in the sacraments, friars who made a sloppy genuflection toward the Blessed Sacrament." Solanus also described Satan as "the prince of diabolical deceivers."

Father Solanus' health worsened in late 1955. He was in pain from a skin disease called erysipelas. Its nickname was St. Anthony's Fire, and it left his skin highly irritated and scaly. He left St. Felix to return to St. Bonaventure Monastery in Detroit in January 1956, where there was hope for finding more highly specialized doctors in the big city. The monastery sought to keep his return quiet so no crowds would bother him with calls and visits. This photograph by Frank Lyerla of the *Detroit Times* shows the friar's weathered hands.

Father Solanus spent weeks in and out of the hospital for treatment. But during periods of renewed vigor, he enjoyed recreation with the friars. Here, he played Scrabble with another Capuchin, Fr. Rudolph Multerer.

Father Solanus bestows a blessing on Albert Sandor, OFM Cap, at the altar of St. Bonaventure Monastery in Detroit in about 1956. Father Sandor was a new seminarian when he met the legendary friar and was inspired by Solanus' persistence in pursuing the priesthood. Sandor, much like Solanus, had difficulties in his seminary studies. For many years, Sandor did cooking and housekeeping work for the Capuchin Friars. "I went down the same path as Solanus because my marks were not high," Sandor has recounted. Solanus told him: "Don't worry, your day will come." He stuck with his studies and was ordained a priest on June 11, 1982. In 2018, when this book was published, he was living and ministering at the Capuchin monastery in Detroit. (Walter P. Reuther Library, Archives of Labor and Urban Affairs, Wayne State University.)

Four

FINAL REST

Father Solanus died on July 31, 1957, at St. John Hospital on Detroit's east side. It was the 53rd anniversary of his first Mass as a Catholic priest at St. Joe's in Appleton, Wisconsin, on July 31, 1904. He had been in the hospital for more than three months, debilitated by the painful skin condition erysipelas. In his last hours, he told Fr. Gerald Walker, OFM Cap, the following: "I looked on my whole life as giving, and I want to give until there is nothing left of me to give. So I prayed that, when I come to die, I might be perfectly conscious, so that with a deliberate act I can give my last breath to God." At 11:00 a.m., those at his bedside reported that Solanus opened his eyes, stretched out his arms, and said, "I give my soul to Jesus Christ." Thousands paid their respects. Visitation was at a nearby funeral home, but the following photographs all were taken on the day of Father Solanus' funeral Mass at St. Bonaventure Monastery in Detroit.

"When people died, Solanus made a point not only to pray for them, but to visit the home, bless the corpse, and console the deceased. . . . Solanus was known to be deeply solicitous of those who died," wrote Fr. Michael Crosby, his Capuchin biographer. A crowd estimated at 8,000 to 10,000 people gathered outside the Detroit monastery to pay their respects.

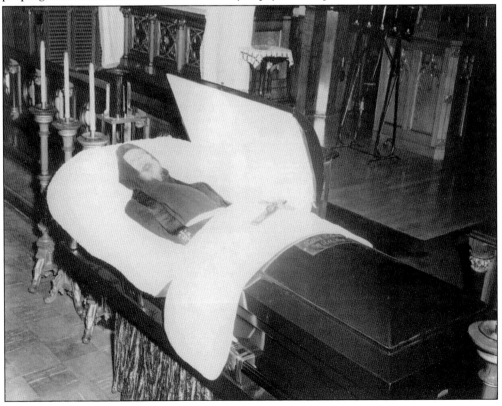

To arrange the visitation, the Capuchins turned to mortician Arthur Van Lerberghe. He had operated a funeral home just a few blocks from St. Bonaventure and became friends with Solanus. In 1937, Van Lerberghe told Solanus he needed capital to build a bigger funeral home and to pray for him to find a way. The next morning, Van Lerberghe reported that an investor called to cosign a $100,000 loan note. In gratitude, Van Lerberghe never charged burial fees for Capuchins.

Visitation at the funeral home was scheduled to run from 1:00 to 10:00 p.m. on August 2, 1957. However, at 5:00 a.m., the line of mourners stretched the length of a city block, and people kept ringing the doorbell to gain entrance. Visitation lasted until 2:00 a.m. the next day, the morning of Father Solanus' funeral at St. Bonaventure.

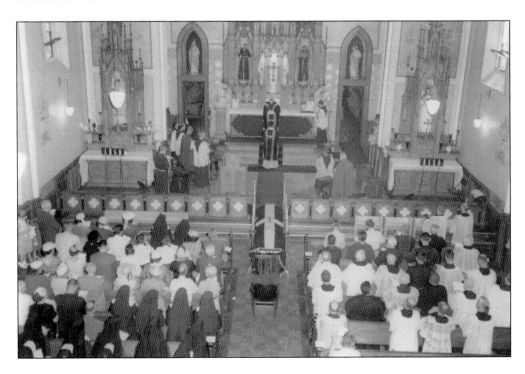

At the funeral Mass, Fr. Gerald Walker, OFM Cap, who looked up to Solanus as a young man and rose to become his superior as the Capuchin provincial, eulogized him as follows: "His was a life of service and love for people like me and you. When he himself was not sick, he nevertheless suffered with and for you that were sick. [When] he was not physically hungry, he hungered with people like you. He had a divine love for people. He loved people for what he could do for them—and for God, through them."

Fr. Gerald Walker, choking back tears during the eulogy, stated, "Father Solanus was a man I loved dearly." As the funeral Mass concluded, the crowd outside prepared to watch a procession of friars, priests, religious sisters, family, and friends walk from St. Bonaventure to the monastery's cemetery gates.

Msgr. Edward Casey, Solanus' brother, celebrated the funeral Mass. Of the 10 boys who once could field an entire baseball team—plus an umpire—in Wisconsin, Edward had become the last living Casey brother. As his brother's casket was carried from the chapel, Monsignor Casey sang the following antiphon: "May the angels lead you into paradise; may the martyrs receive you at your arrival and lead you into the holy city Jerusalem. May the choir of angels receive you."

In this photograph, the procession makes its way into the cemetery. Among those in attendance were several of Father Solanus' relatives who also chose religious vocations. Solanus Casey biographer Catherine M. Odell writes that it was not until Solanus' death that the Capuchins discovered they had recorded the wrong birthdate for the friar: "It was only in preparing death cards and the script for his stone that his proper birthday was discovered. For sixty years, Fr. Solanus had not bothered to 'correct' the Capuchin record, which had long listed his date of birth as October 25 rather than November 25."

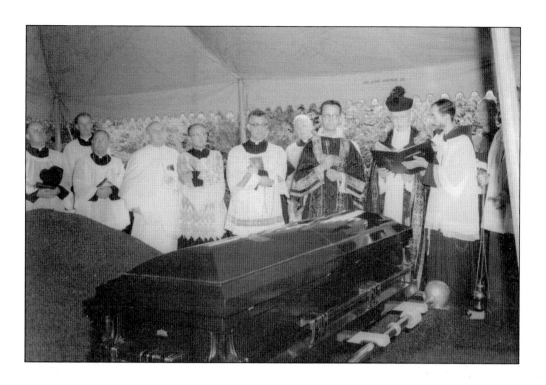

Msgr. Edward Casey, one of Solanus' brothers, gave a final blessing at the gravesite, as pictured above. To Edward's left, Solanus' assistant, Brother Leo Wollenweber, OFM Cap, held open the book of prayer. In the below photograph, religious sisters gather near the casket.

In the above photograph, Detroit's Auxiliary Bishop Henry E. Donnelly, wearing a traditional tufted biretta, stands near the casket of his friend Solanus as a woman wipes tears from her eyes. The priest holding the cross in the photograph is Fr. James Molloy, a Casey family friend who considered Solanus a mentor. Below, mourners pay their final respects.

The crowd slowly filed out of the cemetery, but all walked past the casket one more time to bid a final goodbye.

A simple stone marker was placed on Solanus' grave. It was no different from the others in the cemetery. In the years to come, hundreds came to say a prayer over his grave. "He was a legend before his death; here the legend gains new life," wrote biographer James Patrick Derum.

This is Father Solanus' original gravestone. As part of the Catholic Church's examination of his life for possible sainthood, Solanus' casket was exhumed in 1987, and his remains were examined. The Capuchins prepared a new resting place for his remains, placing a new casket and entombment inside the Capuchin complex and near the chapel, where pilgrims could more readily visit and pray. Reburied below the original gravestone is Father Solanus' original casket. Buried in a plot next to him is Brother Leo Wollenweber, OFM Cap, who led the cause for Solanus' canonization until he himself died in 2012. The bas-relief monument in the cemetery, near where Brother Michael Gaffney, OFM Cap, is standing in the below image, depicts St. Francis of Assisi and words from the "Hymn to the Sun": "Praise to the Lord for our Sister bodily death." (Both, photograph by Diane Weiss.)

Five

"Blessed be God in All His Designs"

One of Father Solanus' favorite sayings was "Blessed be God in all His designs." In the years after his death, his fellow Capuchins, friends, family members, and followers designed many ways to continue Solanus' legacy of service and chart his path to sainthood. More than 60 years after his death, legions of Catholics across the world keep a memento of Fr. Solanus Casey near them—perhaps tucked into a prayer book, a bedside drawer, a wallet, or a pocket. The mementos are Father Solanus relic badges, oval pieces of plastic that encase a photograph of the Capuchin friar along with a pinprick of brown cloth. The pieces are held together by an edging of hand-stitched embroidery. On the badge are the last words uttered by Casey: "I give my soul to Jesus Christ." The badges were started by an extraordinary group of volunteers who, as the fledgling Father Solanus Guild, vowed to keep his memory and outreach alive after his death. The guild has distributed hundreds of thousands of badges for free. Chanel Pattah, 26, a nurse from Orchard Lake, Michigan, said she carries a Solanus Casey badge with her when she is doing nursing rounds. "It's a comfort in my pocket," said Pattah. "If I reach in, it's there and it reminds me of why I'm doing what I'm doing." (Photograph by Patricia Montemurri.)

This relic badge shows signs of how much it is cherished. For decades since his mother gave it to him, University of Detroit Jesuit High School Spanish teacher Paul G. Diehl has carried this with him. The crocheted edges are worn down smooth from the years spent tucked into his wallet. The back of the card notes that the dot of brown cloth came from one of the Capuchin habits worn by Father Solanus before his death in 1957. The badge is considered a second-class relic. Today, the material used to make relic badges is from a brown cloth touched to Solanus' tomb at St. Bonaventure Monastery in Detroit. The current badges are considered third-class relics. (Both, photograph by Patricia Montemurri.)

The Father Solanus Guild maintains offices at St. Bonaventure Monastery, where a display case showcases the tools used to make relic badges. Elenor Geiger, pictured above with her son, punched out plastic ovals in their basement with an electrical press that weighed a few tons. Before that, Father Solanus Guild member Dorothy Fletcher recruited people to cut out the plastic discs one at a time. Today, the Father Solanus Guild employs a die-cutting company to press thousands of pieces per hour. But as the photograph at right shows, making a badge still requires a delicate human touch.

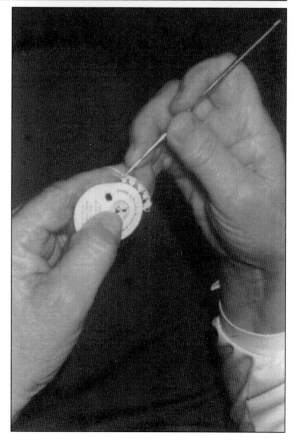

This Father Solanus Guild display illustrates how the badges have changed. The image of Father Solanus now used in badges captures him wearing red-frame glasses and smiling. This image shows the components of badge-making.

FATHER SOLANUS GUILD NEWS

OFFICIAL PUBLICATION - CAUSE OF
VENERABLE SOLANUS CASEY, O.F.M. CAPUCHIN
DETROIT, MICHIGAN

Fr. Solanus Casey
Capuchin

WINTER 2009-2010   VOL. 39, No. 4

THE GUILD TURNS 50 THIS YEAR!

"Solanus Guild History" by Br. Leo Wollenweber

In the beginning, the movement to canonize Fr. Solanus Casey was essentially a lay movement. The friars of the Province didn't think much about canonization for Solanus. But like St. Francis, Fr. Solanus was revered by the people to whom he had devoted his life in service. The group of lay people, some of whom had experienced Solanus' help, expressed an interest in starting a Guild shortly after his death. The Superiors felt that the time was not right and discouraged their plans. In 1960, the subject was revisited and this time, Provincial Minister Gerald Walker and Guardian Rupert Dorn approved.

On May 6, 1960, some 20 people met at the home of Dan and Clare Ryan and formally established the Father Solanus Guild with Fr. Rupert as the first moderator or director. On July 31st of that year, the third anniversary of Fr. Solanus' death, a memorial Mass was held. Afterward, officers were elected and Mrs. Clare Ryan, original promoter of the idea, became the first president. Following as president were

Dorothy Fletcher, Edward Wollenweber, Patrick Blake, and Richard Wollenweber. The purpose of the Guild (as stated in the Constitutions) was to preserve the memory and example of Fr. Solanus and to collect writings and materials concerning his life and work. At the same time, the Guild pledged itself to support the new seminary of St. Mary being built at Crown Point, Indiana, as a memorial to Fr. Solanus. In the next few years the Guild was able to raise thousands of dollars for the seminary.

The Guild continued to ask the province to take up the Cause for Canonization of Fr. Solanus and in 1966, Fr Gerard Hesse, Provincial Minister, sent documents testifying to the holiness of Solanus to the General Minister in Rome. On October 4, 1966, the Postulator General appointed Fr. Paschal Siler as Vice-Postulator. During the next few years, moderator/spiritual director of the Guild was held by several Capuchin friars. In 1973, Roman Hammes and Richard Merling were named Co-Directors. When Hammes left the community, Ignatius Milne joined as co-director until 1979 when his health failed. Since that time, Br. Richard has been Director. Since 1974, Br. Leo Wollenweber has been Vice-Postulator of the Cause.

First card party fundraiser, Cobo Hall, May 19, 1961. Left to right: Dan and Clare Ryan, life-sized photo of Fr. Solanus, and Fr. Rupert Dorn, Guardian of the Monastery (Local Superior) at that time.

Leona Garrity contacted hundreds of people who had stories of Solanus and in 1968, James P. Derum wrote the first biography. In 1961, the Guild had 1,800 members and now counts over 100,000 members in all parts of the world who are praying that Venerable Solanus Casey may soon be declared "Blessed." †

The Father Solanus Guild began through the efforts of Clare Ryan and her husband, Dan, who were friends with Solanus. This 2010 issue of the *Father Solanus Guild News* commemorates the guild's 50th anniversary. The photograph at lower left shows Dan and Clare Ryan along with Fr. Rupert Dorn, OFM Cap, who was the director of the Father Solanus Guild in the 1960s, as they posed with an iconic portrait of Father Solanus. Clare Ryan said Father Solanus' prayers contributed to restoring her health. She said severe arthritis made her bedridden for months. When her husband drove her to the monastery, Father Solanus came out to the car to pray over her. She said she later walked up the stairs at home.

When it was started in 1960, the Father Solanus Guild held meetings in the Third Order Hall, shown on the far left in the above photograph. Next to it is the building where the Capuchin Soup Kitchen was launched. In 10 years, the Father Solanus Guild grew to 5,000 members. The Father Solanus Guild's efforts are credited with initiating, in 1966, the Catholic process, called a cause, to promote the beatification and canonization of Fr. Solanus Casey. The below photograph shows the meeting hall's interior, which also served as a rudimentary museum. One of Solanus' habits is displayed on a table in the foreground.

In the undated photograph shown above, volunteers gathered at the Third Order Hall to sew items for the Capuchin Friars, all while keeping their hats on. Volunteers still provide sewing services, using their skills to repair the friars' habits and other items. Today, nearly 100 volunteers, mostly women, use a crochet hook and fine yarn to put the finishing touches on Father Solanus relic badges. Many say they find the work relaxing and meditative. Josie Strasz of suburban Detroit, pictured below, says she often prays while she crochets. The volunteers buy their own embroidery yarn for the task, which accounts for the wide variety of colors and sheens adorning the badges. (Below, photograph by Patricia Montemurri.)

FATHER SOLANUS GUILD NEWS

OFFICIAL PUBLICATION - CAUSE OF
VENERABLE SOLANUS CASEY, O.F.M. CAPUCHIN
DETROIT, MICHIGAN

Father Solanus Guild
50 Years
1960 - 2010

SUMMER / FALL 2010   VOL. 40, No. 2/3

50th Anniversary of the Fr. Solanus Guild and 53rd Anniversary of the Death of Fr. Solanus

Detroit. The July 23-31 celebration at St. Bonaventure included a 9-Day Novena with daily Mass and a dinner party at The Ark of St. Ambrose July 24th. See Page 5 for more photos.

Guild News Re-Numbered!

Beginning 2011 with Vol. 41, issues will be numbered 1-4 by calendar year. Currently, Issue No. 4 was the Winter issue published in February. For those keeping track, there will be no Vol. 40, No. 4.

New York. The Queen of All Saints Circle of the Solanus Guild celebrated July 31. See photos page 8.

L-R: Fr. Jim Hast, Ass't Director Solanus Center; Br. Leo Wollenweber, Vice Postulator; Br. Richard Merling, Director of the Guild; Fr. Paschal Siler, first Vice Postulator of the Cause; Fr. Rupert Dorn, first Moderator of the Guild; and Fr. Larry Webber, Director of the Center.

Through the Father Solanus Guild's newsletter, its 35,000 members get regular updates about the progress of Fr. Solanus Casey's canonization process. In its first decade of existence, the Father Solanus Guild was credited with collecting hundreds of letters and cards penned by Father Solanus. Its members interviewed more than 200 people about their experiences with Father Solanus and chronicled them to prepare the cause for his possible sainthood. This edition celebrated the Father Solanus Guild's 50 anniversary in 2010.

The testimony collected by the Father Solanus Guild was incorporated into a 3,600-page document called the *Positio*. It is an exhaustive biography of Father Solanus, and it was prepared, in part, by Fr. Michael Crosby, OFM Cap. Crosby died on August 5, 2017, at age 77. The *Positio* was reviewed by the Vatican's Congregation for the Causes of Saints. The congregation determined that Father Solanus was an example of "heroic virtue" and "uncommon holiness," which led to Pope John Paul II bestowing the title of "Venerable" upon Father Solanus in 1995.

Br. Richard Merling (left) and Br. Leo Wollenweber presented the Solanus Icon Plaque to Pope John Paul II to personally thank him for declaring Solanus "Venerable."

To thank Pope John Paul II for bestowing the title of "Venerable" on Father Solanus, the Capuchins gave the pontiff a plaque depicting the Capuchin priest. Greeting the pope were Brothers Leo Wollenweber (center) and Richard Merling (left), two Detroit-born Capuchins who knew Father Solanus.

Brother Leo Wollenweber was a fledgling Capuchin when he worked as the secretary to Father Solanus for five years at St. Bonaventure Monastery. For more than three decades after Solanus' death, Brother Leo's job was to investigate Father Solanus' life and chronicle reports of unexplained healings in the hunt for a miracle. He passed away on October 5, 2012, at age 95. Here, he is shown in a reflective moment inside St. Bonaventure Monastery chapel.

FATHER SOLANUS GUILD NEWS

OFFICIAL PUBLICATION - CAUSE OF
VENERABLE SOLANUS CASEY, O.F.M. CAPUCHIN
DETROIT, MICHIGAN

FALL 2012

VOL. 42, No. 3/4

Remembering Br. Leo

Br. Leo Wollenweber, OFM Capuchin, Vice Postulator for the Cause of Solanus Casey, entered eternal life October 5, 2012 at the age of 95. Br. Leo made his First Profession May 18, 1941. Three years later his Solemn Profession fell on the same day, May 18, 1944.

Br. Leo is a native of Detroit who lived and worked with Solanus at the monastery office for five years. In 1946, Br. Leo was appointed instructor in the Brothers' Novitiate and served as Assistant Novice Director for the next 14 years in Detroit, Milwaukee and Mt. Calvary WI. He returned to Saint Bonaventure as porter for the next 11 years, then served on the retreat team at the Capuchin Retreat House in Washington, MI for eight years. Br. Leo designed the Stations of the Cross there, the monument for the tomb of Solanus, and many other artworks around the Province. Br. Leo was appointed Vice Postulator for the Cause of Solanus Casey in 1974 and his biography, *Meet Solanus Casey,* was published in 2002 *(see page 10 for ordering info)*. Br. Leo once said, "The example and inspiration of Venerable Solanus has indeed been a perfect model of St. Francis which has sustained me throughout these long and happy years as a Capuchin Brother." The background of this page is just one of the many watercolor paintings Br. Leo left as part of his legacy. May he now rest in peace. ✝

This issue of the *Father Solanus Guild News* followed Brother Leo Wollenweber's death in 2012. The issue depicts Brother Leo with other members of the guild staff. At the bottom right corner of the page, staffers celebrated Brother Leo's 95th birthday at the guild office inside St. Bonaventure Monastery.

Father Solanus' legacy is reflected in the dependable outreach of the Capuchin Soup Kitchen. Founded during the Great Depression, the Capuchin Soup Kitchen outgrew the original building, pictured here, where Father Solanus ladled out soup. The buildings once used by the Father Solanus Guild and the soup kitchen were bulldozed around 2001 to make way for the Solanus Casey Center. There are now two Capuchin Soup Kitchen sites, including a modern facility around the corner from St. Bonaventure. The Capuchin Soup Kitchen also offers programs to help people rebuild their lives after prison or addiction, as well as to enhance learning opportunities for children.

Entertainer and comedian Danny Thomas, who was born in Michigan and started his show business career in Detroit, headlined a Capuchin Soup Kitchen fundraiser in 1955. He starred in the television sitcom *Make Room for Daddy* (later called *The Danny Thomas Show*) from 1953 to 1965 and was the founder of St. Jude Children's Research Hospital in Memphis, Tennessee. It is unclear if the actor and Father Solanus ever met.

Aldo Mastro, a longtime Ford Motor Company employee, worked tirelessly to build community support and sell tickets to annual fundraisers for the Capuchin Soup Kitchen. The annual Support Our Capuchin Kitchen (SOCK) dinner regularly draws up to 1,000 attendees. An award named after Mastro is presented annually to the top ticket seller. The elder Aldo Mastro (seated at far left) brought his son, Aldo P. Mastro (seated at center), and his brother, Lauro Mastro (seated at right), to a Capuchin fundraiser in 1970. Joining them were his son's classmates from University of Detroit Jesuit High School; they are, from left to right, Jim Diehl, David Schafer, Paul Diehl, Frank DiLaura, and Kevin Lavey. (Mastro family.)

Since 1977, Detroit-area restaurant chain Buddy's Pizza has set aside a "Slice for Life" day to raise money for the Capuchin Soup Kitchen. Folks buy tickets at the doors of Buddy's Pizza locations for all-you-can-eat pizza and salad, and the proceeds benefit the Capuchin Soup Kitchen. Pictured here with unidentified supporters (and pizza-lovers) is the late Fr. Lloyd Thiel (center), who was director of the Capuchin Soup Kitchen for 14 years.

The two Capuchin Soup Kitchen (CSK) facilities serve about 60,000 meals and 250,000 pounds of food monthly. Brother Nick Blattner, OFM Cap (left), and a guest meet at the Meldrum Street kitchen. The charity provides more than food. Other programs affiliated with the CSK provide educational programs to children and assistance for people recovering from addiction. CSK also promotes organic farming and earth-friendly initiatives. (Photograph by Phillip Gardner.)

Six

WONDERS, FAVORS, AND A MIRACLE

Many have stories about how Blessed Solanus Casey's prayers or presence brought them comfort, strength, and relief from physical and mental pain. During his life, he was known as a wonder-worker and spiritual healer. Father Solanus recorded some of these accounts in a ledger, which was unearthed nine years after his death, of people who called or wrote to thank him for unexplained healings or prayers answered. But there is a rigorous, exhaustive procedure that takes place in order for the Roman Catholic Church to determine that a miracle has occurred. All the reported healings attributed to Solanus during his lifetime did not make him a saint in the eyes of the church. Instead, the Vatican's saint-makers required that a miracle occur after the candidate's death for beatification to occur. Once a candidate is beatified, yet another church-recognized miracle healing must occur for the candidate to be considered for sainthood. Here are some stories from the faithful who say Father Solanus' prayers blessed, helped, or healed loved ones. Joyce Karwowicz, of Warren, Michigan, said her mother, Theresa Frydrych Janowski, had eye problems that were cured after a visit to Solanus. Joyce was married at St. Bonaventure Monastery and cherishes this photograph of her parents and husband from that day. (Photograph by Brett Karwowicz.)

Kelly Maher (left), who grew up in Grosse Pointe, Michigan, was born 13 weeks premature, and her mother, Gloria Louwers, was told that she would not live through the night. Louwers had met the friar as a child. Kelly rallied after a Casey relic was placed in her isolette. (Photograph by Paul G. Diehl.)

Siblings Kathy Miller and Gary Kudron, of suburban Detroit, cherish a photograph of their late mother, Jean Kudron. Jean had severe ulcerative colitis, and Father Solanus prayed with her at St. Bonaventure in 1956. "Jean lived with the determination to be healed and the hope that she could endure her situation," said Gary. "We believe that our mother had a long, beautiful, and inspirational life due to the blessing of Fr. Solanus Casey." (Photograph by Paul G. Diehl.)

When Anne Marie Ufford became a nun with the Sisters, Servants of the Immaculate Heart of Mary (IHM) congregation in Monroe, she took the religious name Sr. Mary Solanus. Her aunt's husband, Ed Karber, who had adopted Anne and three orphaned siblings, converted to Catholicism after becoming friends with Father Solanus. (SSIHM Archives.)

Father Solanus' gifts did not always bring healings but sometimes prophecy. Sr. Raymonda Trudeau visited Father Solanus with another IHM nun who requested prayers for health. Father Solanus told the one sister that she would be fine, but explained to Sister Raymonda that she would face a life of suffering. Some years later, Sister Raymonda was disabled by painful, deforming arthritis and spent more than 30 years living in the infirmary. Through her suffering, she remained prayerful and offered it up to God. She died in 1982 at age 83. (SSIHM Archives.)

Molly Towne, of St. Clement Parish in Saratoga Springs, New York, was born limp and with no discernible heartbeat in 1984. Doctors rushed to resuscitate her. Her mother, Susanne Towne, placed a Solanus Casey badge in her daughter's isolette. Molly recovered, and as an adult, she participated in Solanus' beatification ceremony in 2017. She is pictured here with Albany's Bishop Edward Scharfenberger. (The *Evangelist*; photograph by Kate Blain.)

When George Taylor was going blind, he regularly came to the weekly Blessing of the Sick service held at St. Bonaventure Monastery in Detroit. Even though he was not cured, he told his children, Joseph and Jessica, that he believed his prayers at Solanus' tomb brought him solace and tranquility. (Photograph by Brother Michael Gaffney, OFM Cap.)

John Ahee credits prayer to Father Solanus for surviving a rare brain cancer that struck in 1996. Ahee said days before he was to start chemotherapy in 1996, a high-ranking Catholic Church official prayed to Father Solanus and told Ahee to try another treatment. Ahee's story was part of a video presentation at Fr. Solanus Casey's beatification ceremony. (Archdiocese of Detroit; photograph by Tim Hinkle.)

As a severely ill baby, Dennis Lukasik was brought to the door of St. Bonaventure Monastery to be blessed by Fr. Solanus Casey. For years now, he has come to Saturday morning Mass at the monastery with his buddies to pray anew. Pictured are, from left to right, Bill Axtell, Art Formella, Lukasik, Gary Dietz, and Dave Leonard. (Photograph by Patricia Montemurri.)

Rosellen Loye-Bucy recounted to the *Michigan Catholic* the story of when Father Solanus brought this relic on a visit to her ailing father in the 1940s. "[He reached] into his deep pocket and [brought] out a large silver disk with a glass cover [and] let me touch it and [explained] that in the center was a relic of the True Cross surrounded by a relic of each of the Twelve apostles." The Capuchins in Detroit use the relic in healing services to this day. (*Detroit Free Press*; photograph by Eric Seals)

Every Wednesday, for nearly 100 years, the Capuchins in Detroit have held a weekly Blessing of the Sick service. Here, Fr. George Kooran prays for Sidney Davis. Davis has found faith and friendship at the monastery for more than 10 years. "I know if it wasn't for them," he says of the Capuchins and their staff, "there wouldn't be me." (Photograph by Diane Weiss.)

In the above photograph, Brother Anthony Kote-Witah, OFM Cap, offers the comfort of touch and a blessing to an attendee at a weekly Wednesday healing service at the monastery. For years, pilgrims have come to Father Solanus' tomb and left written prayer requests on top of it. Every night, the Capuchins place the notes in a basket at the chapel altar, offer prayers, and then burn them. (Above, photograph by Brother Michael Gaffney, OFM Cap; below, *Michigan Catholic*; photograph by Michael Stechschulte.)

Paula Medina Zarate was a schoolteacher in Panama who also volunteered at Catholic parishes run by Detroit-based Capuchin priests near Panama City. She had suffered her entire life with ichthyosis, a genetic skin condition that caused the development of thick, fishlike scales all over her body. Her skin cracked and bled, and Panama's heat only intensified the irritation and pain. She visited the Capuchin monastery in Detroit in 2012 and knelt at Father Solanus' tomb. She first prayed for others, but heard a voice tell her to pray for herself. Within minutes of kneeling and praying at the tomb, her skin began to clear, and dried scales fell off her legs in sheets. Doctors in Detroit, Panama, and from the Vatican tested her and reviewed medical records and determined there was no medical explanation for her skin to clear. Pope Francis declared that a miracle occurred through the intercession of Fr. Solanus Casey.

Paula Medina Zarate and her Panamanian dermatologist visited Detroit so church and medical experts could investigate her condition. Zarate was examined by three metro Detroit dermatologists, including an expert on ichthyosis, and biopsies were taken of her skin. Medical experts, including Detroit-area dermatologist Dr. Lisa Manz-Dulac, pictured above (at right) with Zarate, concluded Zarate still has the genetic skin condition, but the miraculous healing is that the disease does not "manifest itself." Below, the medical experts' findings are sealed with red wax before being delivered to the Vatican by the Capuchin general postulator, Fr. Carlo Carloni, OFM Cap. Pictured below are, from left to right, Carloni, Detroit's Archbishop Allen Vigneron, and Capuchins Larry Webber and Richard Merling.

Before the beatification, Detroit Catholic officials exhumed Father Solanus' remains from his tomb in the monastery to obtain a few fragments of bone to create relics for public display. The church uses relics as a symbol of faith. Above, a crew of workers, which includes excavation experts and Capuchins in street clothes, poses with the removed vault. Brother Jerry Johnson, OFM Cap, left, and funeral home director Brian Joseph, right, are pictured below. (Both, *Michigan Catholic*; photographs by Michael Stechshulte.)

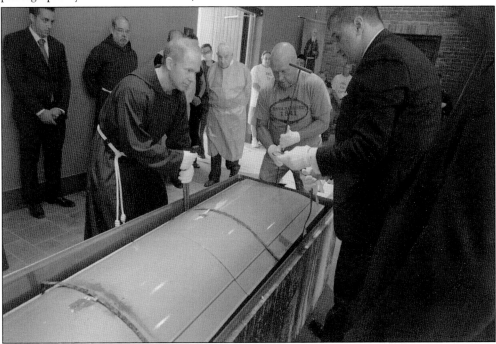

Above, Archbishop Allen Vigneron inspects the remains of Fr. Solanus Casey after they were exhumed in September 2017. Afterward, he spent some quiet moments in reflection and prayer, as shown below. During the night, Capuchin friars took turns staying with Solanus' casket before his remains could be interred into a refurbished tomb at St. Bonaventure. (Both, *Michigan Catholic*; photographs by Michael Stechshulte.)

FM Solanus Casey, OFM Cap

Born
November 25, 1870

Invested
January 14, 1897

Perpetually Professed
July 21, 1901

Ordained
July 24, 1904

Died
July 31, 1957

Declared Venerable
July 11, 1995

Beatified
November 18, 2017

A new tomb was designed for Blessed Solanus Casey's remains. The design reveals the casket's shiny black exterior, with an engraved likeness of Solanus' face and script that details the basic facts of his life and the titles bestowed on him by the Roman Catholic Church as his sainthood cause advances. (*Michigan Catholic*; photograph by Michael Stechschulte.)

Under Catholic Church rules, only statues of people declared a saint or "blessed" are allowed inside the sanctuary. On the day before his Beatification Mass, this life-size sculpture of Blessed Solanus, the doorkeeper of St. Bonaventure Monastery, awaited its move through the church doors. (Photograph by Patricia Montemurri.)

Seven

THE BLESSING
OF BEATIFICATION

On November 18, 2017, some 66,000 people gathered at Detroit's Ford Field to witness the Beatification Mass that decreed Fr. Solanus Casey as "Blessed" and a miracle worker. It was only the third time that the Catholic rite of beatification had been celebrated on American soil and was the largest Catholic Mass ever held in the city of Detroit. (*Detroit Free Press*; photograph by Junfu Han.)

The rainy, stormy weather did not deter the faithful, who had to snake through metal detectors to gain entrance to the home of the National Football League's Detroit Lions. Free tickets to the Beatification Mass were snatched up within a day of release. Nearly 400 buses transported Catholics from area parishes to the event. Inside the arena, the mood before the Beatification Mass was festive. Among the lighthearted touches were paper fans emblazoned with a whimsical cartoon drawing of Father Solanus wearing red-rimmed glasses. (Above, photograph by Sean G. Work; below, *Detroit Free Press*; photograph by Ryan Garza.)

Inside the stadium, 200 Catholic priests set up pop-up confessionals in the hallways. Many Catholics stood in line to confess their sins and partake in the sacrament of penance. (*Michigan Catholic*; photograph by Jeff Kowalsky.)

The *Michigan Catholic*, the biweekly newspaper of the Archdiocese of Detroit, gave away souvenir copies of a special edition celebrating Blessed Solanus Casey. (*Detroit Free Press*; photograph by Ryan Garza.)

Graphic designer Cassandra Ewert created shareable cartoon emojis of Father Solanus suitable for social media and to accompany the Twitter hashtag #BlessedSolanus. Phillip Gardner, the Capuchins' social media manager, said the cartoon images are figures "we might not see in the traditional icons of saints, but move us all to be everyday saints."

Nearly 300 Capuchin friars from around the world came to Detroit for the beatification. In the right foreground, Brother Rob Roemer, OFM Cap, of Milwaukee, holds a fan displaying an emoji-like depiction of Father Solanus. (*Michigan Catholic*; photograph by Jeff Kowalsky.)

Pilgrims came from around the United States and the world. Among them were members of the Vietnamese Eucharistic Youth Movement, who traveled to Detroit from throughout the Midwest and Washington, DC, area. Their red-and-yellow scarves feature the colors of the Vietnamese flag. (Photograph by M.J. Groark, OFM Cap.)

This sign reserved some 300 seats on the main floor for the Casey clan, relatives of Blessed Solanus Casey. Sr. Mary Vianney, who is holding the sign, is a member of the Marian Sisters of Santa Rosa congregation in California. She traveled to the Beatification Mass with Sr. Caritas Marie Cunningham, who is the great-great-granddaughter of Margaret Casey LeDoux, one of Solanus' sisters. (Brett Mountain Photography.)

Some 300 members of Blessed Solanus Casey's extended family travelled from Ireland and all over the United States to Detroit for the Beatification Mass. Solanus' great-niece, Sr. Anne Herkenrath, a Catholic nun from Seattle, helped track descendants with color-coded name tags. Solanus Casey, born with the name of Bernard Francis (named after his father), was one of 16 siblings. Two sisters died in childhood, and two other siblings became priests. Descendants of eight of Solanus' siblings were at the ceremony. A contingent also came from Ireland—relatives of Solanus' Irish-born parents. Blessed Solanus reportedly has 3,000 relatives over 10 generations, tracked by a family member in Ireland who became a professional genealogist while researching the family tree. Over the years, various relatives visited Detroit for ceremonies marking anniversaries of Solanus' passing or other events, but never had so many of the Capuchin's relatives gathered

in such large number. Relatives in attendance ranged in age from octogenarians to six-month-old Chase Kosoglow of San Jose, California, who is seated on the lap of his mother, Kate Schneider Kosoglow, in the first row of chairs. Chase's dad, Richard Kosoglow, is seated next to Kate and Chase. Chase's great-great-grandmother was Genevieve Casey McCluskey, Solanus' youngest sister. Sister Herkenrath, seated second from the right in the first row of chairs, is the Casey clan's unofficial leader and spokesperson. She keeps distant family members abreast of developments and is a frequent visitor to Detroit. Herkenrath, a member of the Sisters of the Holy Names of Jesus and Mary, represented the Casey family when Blessed Solanus Casey was inducted into the Irish American Hall of Fame at the Irish American Heritage Center in Chicago in April 2018. (Brett Mountain Photography.)

From left to right in the first row, Fr. Larry Webber, OFM Cap; Brother Richard Merling, OFM Cap; and Brother Michael Sullivan, OFM Cap, await the start of the beatification. Seated next to Sullivan is Paula Medina Zarate, whose skin disease was cured after she prayed at Father Solanus' tomb. Webber and Merling were co–vice postulators for promoting Blessed Solanus' cause for sainthood. Sullivan heads the Capuchin Franciscan Province of St. Joseph, which stretches from Montana to the Midwest. (*Michigan Catholic*; photograph by Jeff Kowalsky.)

Cardinal Joseph Tobin, the first Detroit-born-and-bred priest to become a Catholic cardinal, participated in the beatification. He heads the archdiocese in Newark, New Jersey. His sister Gerarda Tobin (left) helped coordinate the beatification ceremony, and her husband, Brian Joseph, is on the right. Blessed Solanus, said Cardinal Tobin, "is a Detroit saint, and he speaks to every Detroiter, and the ones who are looked over or forgotten." (Photograph by Patricia Montemurri.)

The choir was led by Fr. Edward Foley, OFM Cap, pictured here, and brought together singers from the Detroit Archdiocesan Choir, the Solanus Casey Center choir, and from parishes across metro Detroit. (*Michigan Catholic*; photograph by Jeff Kowalsky.)

Kevin Coupe, of Kansas City, Missouri, adorned his Solanus Casey relic badge with charms for the Detroit Lions and a fiddle, which represented the friar's violin playing. "He was a poor man, a humble man," Coupe told the *Detroit Free Press*. "In the world today, people need to be humble." (*Detroit Free Press*; photograph by Ryan Garza.)

The procession to begin the Mass included five Catholic cardinals, thirty-five bishops, and dozens of priests, deacons, and seminarians. The entrance hymn was "Festival Canticle" by Richard Hillert. The following words are from the song: "This is the feast of victory for our God. / Alleluia." The purple floor runners shaped like a cross anchored the visual focus of the crowd. (Above, *Michigan Catholic*; photograph by Jeff Kowalsky; below, *Detroit Free Press*; photograph by Junfu Han.)

Brother Richard Merling, second from left, was a child when he met Father Solanus and, as a Capuchin, has been a coleader in the cause for his sainthood. A portrait of Solanus is draped on the platform. Merling recalled that Solanus often said, "I have two loves, the sick and the poor." (Photograph by M.J. Groark, OFM Cap.)

Cardinal Angelo Amato, the prefect for the Vatican's Congregation for the Causes of Saints, was the main celebrant. He drew chuckles when he brought up that Solanus' fellow friars concluded that "Father Solanus was a bad musician." So, Casey would play the violin in a chapel since "the Lord listened to him patiently because our 'Blessed' was lacking in music, but not in virtue." (*Michigan Catholic*; photograph by Jeff Kowalsky.)

Cardinal Angelo Amato read out loud, in Latin, an Apostolic Letter from Pope Francis, while Archbishop Allen Vigneron recited the English version. The church decrees, said Vigneron, "that the venerable servant of god, Francis Solanus, known in the world as Bernard Casey . . . a humble and faithful disciple of Christ, tireless in serving the poor . . . henceforth be called by the name of Blessed." Amato unveiled the iconic portrait of Blessed Solanus and also wafted ceremonial incense over the friar's relic. In his sermon, Cardinal Amato said that Solanus had a "profound faith [which] allowed him to receive others as a brother, independently of their race or religion. Rabbis and ministers of at least 16 Protestant congregations visited him often for discussion and advice." Amato added: "His favorite sons were the poor, the sick, the emarginated, and the homeless. He always fasted in order to give them their own lunch. He spent hours upon hours patiently receiving, listening to, and counseling the ever-growing number of people who came to him. Practically speaking, the greater part of his time as Porter was dedicated to others—from nine o'clock in the morning until nine at night, almost without interruption." (*Detroit Free Press*; photograph by Mandi Wright.)

The altar used for the Beatification Mass was used by St. John Paul II in 1987 when he celebrated Mass for 90,000 people at the Pontiac Silverdome. The altar, designed by architect Gunnar Birkerts, is owned by Tom Monaghan, who founded Domino's Pizza. The altar was designed to evoke the base of a sturdy tree anchoring the ground. It is made of layered cherrywood and is 12 feet long. (Photograph by M.J. Groark, OFM, Cap.)

Holding the Bible aloft is Deacon Jason Graves, OFM Cap. The day's Gospel was taken from Luke 11:10: "And I tell you, ask and you will receive, seek and you will find; knock and the door will be opened to you." (Photograph by M.J. Groark, OFM Cap.)

The prayers of the faithful were recited in Vietnamese, Chaldean, Polish, Tagalog, Spanish, and English. Speaking here is Sr. Anne Bosserman, of the Sisters of the Holy Names of Jesus and Mary. Among the others who delivered prayers were Brother Faris Najor, OFM Cap; Sam Bright; Naim Edwards; and Tramy Vo. (Photograph by M.J. Groark, OFM Cap.)

In the offertory procession of the Catholic Mass, gifts are brought to the altar. Holding a basket of everyday food items is Onakapoma Moore. To her left is Maryann Kummer. Behind them are Brother Anthony Kote-Witah, OFM Cap (left), and Dennis Till. (Photograph by M.J. Groark, OFM Cap.)

In the center foreground, Patrick McGlinnen (left) and his brother Michael participate in the offertory procession. Their mother, Lory McGlinnen, guides them from behind, and their father Michael is to the far left. (Photograph by M.J. Groark, OFM Cap.)

Twin siblings Gianna Johnson and Casey Johnson bring flowers to the altar during the offertory procession. The twins' parents, Michael and Cathi Johnson of Hillsborough County, Florida, said they were able to conceive the children after prayers to Father Solanus. (Photograph by M.J. Groark, OFM Cap.)

Tears ran down the face of Paula Medina Zarate (above, center), the retired Panamanian schoolteacher whose skin disease disappeared after she prayed at Solanus' tomb in Detroit. The pope decreed her healing a miracle. She carried a wood cross to the altar; the cross was adorned with a reliquary containing a bone fragment from Blessed Solanus' remains, as shown below in a close-up of the center of the cross. (Above, *Detroit Free Press*; photograph by Ryan Garza; below, photograph by M.J. Groark, OFM Cap.)

"Detroit is the place of my dreamings now," said Paula Medina Zarate (center) about the miracle. "I feel the desire to be here because I had the healing of my body here, my heart here, and my soul here." She is accompanied by Capuchin Friars Jozef Timmers (left) and Michael Sullivan. (*Detroit Free Press*; photograph by Mandi Wright.)

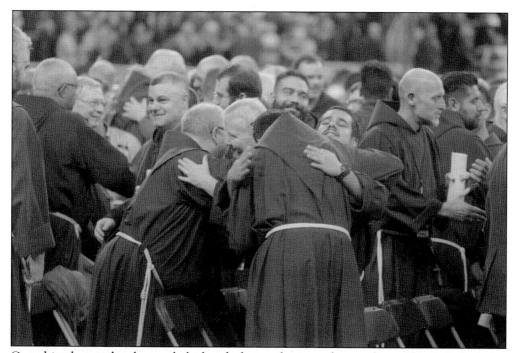

Capuchins hug each other or shake hands during the sign of peace during the Catholic Mass. Many greet each other with the phrase, "Peace be with you." (*Detroit Free Press*; photograph by Ryan Garza.)

Fr. Wolfgang Pisa, originally of Tanzania, readies himself to distribute Holy Communion to Catholics during the Beatification Mass. About 389 Catholic priests and deacons fanned out through the crowd of 66,000 to distribute the Sacrament of the Eucharist. (*Detroit Free Press*; photograph by Ryan Garza.)

Archbishop Allen Vigneron, the spiritual leader of an estimated 1.3 million Catholics in the six-county Archdiocese of Detroit, passes out Communion during the Beatification Mass. (*Michigan Catholic*; photograph by Jeff Kowalsky.)

The Eucharistic Hymn, "Gift of Finest Wheat," was played by an orchestra featuring 20 different instruments. Coleman Ward, the music director at Nativity of Our Lord Parish in Detroit, also sang a solo, the hymn "Taste and See." (*Detroit Free Press*; photograph by Ryan Garza.)

Miracle recipient Paula Medina Zarate hugs Jimmy Gavin. Jimmy's great-aunt Mary Seguin Farmer was a personal friend to Blessed Solanus and drove him on errands. Behind Jimmy is his father, Jim Gavin. (Photograph by Suzanne Gavin.)

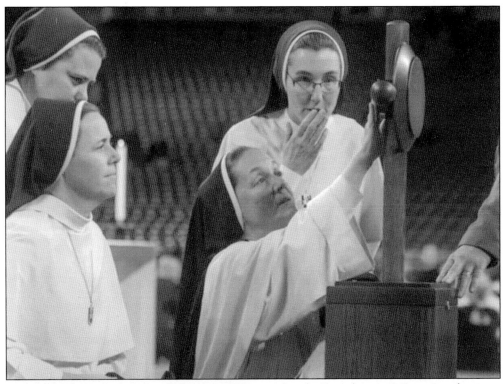

After the Beatification Mass, several nuns reverently approach the cross containing the relic of Blessed Solanus Casey. The sisters are members of the Ann Arbor–based congregation Dominican Sisters of Mary, Mother of the Eucharist. Touching the relic is Sr. Maria Gemma, and standing behind her is Sr. Maria Rose. In the lower left corner is Sr. Maria Faustina, and behind her is Sr. Maximilian Marie. (*Detroit Free Press*; photograph by Ryan Garza.)

This participant's reaction mirrored the delight of those who attended the ceremony. Blessed Solanus Casey's beatification was only the third time such a ceremony was held in the United States. Blessed Sr. Teresa Demjanovich, a New Jersey–born nun who died in 1927, was beatified on October 4, 2014. Blessed Fr. Stanley Rother, a missionary priest who was murdered in Guatemala in 1981, was beatified in Oklahoma City on September 23, 2017. (Photograph by Sean G. Work.)

Eight

CENTERED ON SOLANUS

As Blessed Solanus Casey welcomed all those who came to the door, so does St. Bonaventure Monastery Chapel and the Solanus Casey Center in Detroit. Solanus' beatification has heightened fascination with the friar and with the Capuchin Order's commitment to serving those in physical and spiritual need. The beatification brought some immediate changes in how Blessed Solanus is represented in Catholic institutions, liturgy, and prayer. Blessed Solanus' Catholic feast day is July 30. It is the eve of the day he died—July 31, 1957. That means feast day Masses can be celebrated for Solanus in Capuchin-run churches around the world as well as in the Archdiocese of Detroit and other Catholic dioceses where he lived or ministered in Wisconsin, Indiana, Minnesota, and New York. (Photograph by Diane Weiss.)

He is in! This sculpture of Fr. Solanus Casey could not be placed inside the chapel at St. Bonaventure Monastery until he was beatified. The Catholic Church allows only images of saints and "blessed" individuals inside the sanctuary. However, through a loophole, an image of Fr. Solanus had been inside the chapel for several years. Brother Michael Gaffney, OFM Cap, did a painting that recreated a 1935 meeting in Detroit between Solanus and St. Andre Bessette, a Quebec religious brother who was canonized in 2010. Since Bessette's image is allowed in the sanctuary because he is a saint, Casey's likeness may be included as a secondary image. The Blessed Solanus statue and the cross that contains a bone fragment relic from Solanus' remains can be found at the back of the monastery chapel. (*Michigan Catholic*; photograph by Michael Stechschulte.)

The "loophole" painting of St. Andre Bessette and Blessed Solanus still adorns a back wall inside the chapel at St. Bonaventure. The artist, Brother Michael Gaffney (pictured), has created images of Solanus in various mediums. (Photograph by Diane Weiss.)

Blessed Solanus Casey practiced his ministry every time he opened a door at Capuchin monasteries. Outside St. Bonaventure in Detroit, his likeness stands watch over Mount Elliott Street. (Photograph by Diane Weiss.)

In 2002, the Capuchins dedicated the Solanus Casey Center, a museum and meeting place where guests can learn about the beloved friar. It occupies the land where the original Capuchin Soup Kitchen and Third Order Hall once stood. It was designed to serve the increasing number of people curious about how and where Blessed Solanus Casey lived. A garden greets visitors with a sculpture that symbolize elements of earth and space. The outside shines brightly inside the center, too. (Above, photograph by Brother Michael Gaffney, OFM Cap; below, photograph by Diane Weiss.)

Fr. David Preuss is the director of the Solanus Casey Center. The center contains artifacts from Blessed Solanus' life, including his violin. The center also contains statues and symbols representing other faith practices, such as African American, Protestant, Japanese, and Muslim traditions, among others. Preuss sees the Solanus Casey Center as an oasis from the pressures of the daily hustle and bustle. The center also offers visitors an opportunity to meet with a priest to receive the Catholic Sacrament of Penance. Preuss said Capuchin friars at St. Bonaventure hear about 22,000 confessions each year. (Photograph by Brother Michael Gaffney, OFM Cap.)

There is an open-air outline of a small chapel in the middle of the Solanus Casey Center. It recreates the framework of the original chapel the Capuchins erected in Detroit in 1883. That original chapel, pictured at left, sat in Mount Elliott Cemetery across the street from St. Bonaventure. (Above, photograph by Patricia Montemurri.)

The Solanus Casey Center celebrates the lives of other virtuous people. Inside the front door are eight life-size bronze statues of people whose lives were examples of service, sacrifice, and mercy. They include Catholic social activist Dorothy Day; Msgr. Clement Kern, a Detroit priest; St. Teresa of Calcutta; lay Catholic missionary Jean Donovan and a child; El Salvador's Bishop Oscar Romero, canonized a saint on October 14, 2018; civil rights leader Dr. Martin Luther King Jr.; and Takashi Nagai, a Catholic physician who survived the atomic bomb in Nagasaki, Japan. (Both, photograph by Patricia Montemurri.)

This exhibit at the Solanus Casey Center recreates Father Solanus' room at St. Bonaventure Monastery. Some of the other friars who knew him said that he sometimes slept on the hard bedsprings without a mattress. The display also shows a few of his cherished items, including a harmonica. (Photograph by Brother Michael Gaffney, OFM Cap.)

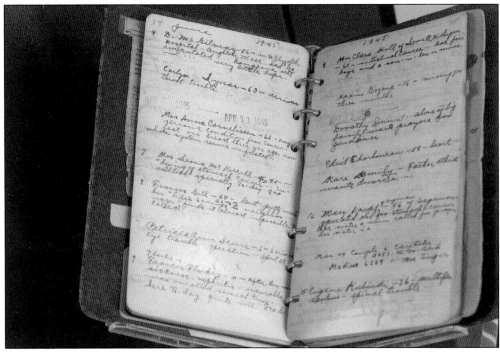

One of Father Solanus' many notebooks, in which he chronicled his visitors and their requests, is on display at the Solanus Casey Center. (Photograph by Diane Weiss.)

The Solanus Casey Center regularly offers tours. On this day, schoolchildren from All Saints Catholic School in Canton, Michigan, gather around the tomb of Blessed Solanus Casey. For his beatification, the casket was made more visible to pilgrims. (Photograph by Brother Michael Gaffney, OFM Cap.)

At the Solanus Casey Center, it is possible to run into a Capuchin who knew Blessed Solanus. These Capuchins lived or served with the virtuous friar. Pictured in this February 2017 photograph are, from left to right, Fr. Pius Cotter, Brother Richard Merling, Fr. Dan Crosby, Fr. Werner Wolf, Fr. David Preuss, and Fr. Brian Braun. (*Michigan Catholic*; photograph by Dan Meloy.)

Below, young people have come to learn more about Blessed Solanus Casey through the Tap into Life program, which meets at St. Bonaventure. At least once a year, Fr. Solanus Casey walks a Detroit street again. He is a fixture as a "Big Head" marcher in Detroit's annual Thanksgiving Parade. In 2017, Fr. Tom Nyugen, pictured at left, who led the Tap into Life program from 2014 to 2018, was under the papier-mâché character of Blessed Solanus on Woodward Avenue. In the below photograph, Tap into Life participants gather at the monastery chapel after a Sunday meeting. (Left, photograph by Patricia Montemurri; below, photograph by Brother Michael Gaffney, OFM Cap.)

In the Seattle cemetery where Blessed Solanus' parents are buried is a monument that carries his likeness and describes his legacy. (Sr. Anne Herkenrath.)

Brother Richard Merling, left, and Fr. Larry Webber, center, the co–vice postulators for Blessed Solanus' cause for sainthood, greeted Pope Francis in Vatican Square in May 2018. They brought him a donation for charity from contributions collected at the Beatification Mass for Blessed Solanus. (*L'Osservatore Romano.*)

As they did when Blessed Solanus was alive, the sacraments of the Catholic Church bring joy and solace to the faithful at St. Bonaventure. Above, Fr. Larry Webber, OFM Cap, baptizes a baby. Below, pilgrims reach out to each other in prayer other over the tomb of Blessed Solanus Casey. In August 2018, the Capuchins began a renovation of the St. Bonaventure Monastery Chapel. The refurbishing was intended to add more seating to the sanctuary as well as restore some features that existed when Blessed Solanus Casey lived and worked at the monastery. The removal of a fake wall provided space to re-create a side chapel and altar dedicated to the Sacred Heart of Jesus. (Above, photograph by Brother Michael Gaffney, OFM Cap; below, photograph by Diane Weiss.)

At the tomb of Blessed Solanus Casey, people find comfort, grace, hope and friendship. In the above photograph, Mack Arther Betts lifts his rosary aloft over the tomb. He is a regular visitor to weekly services. "Blessing of the Sick" services are held at 2:00 p.m. every Wednesday and Sunday. (Both, photograph by Diane Weiss.)

For several days in late July 2018, there were special Masses and events to celebrate the first Feast Day of Blessed Solanus Casey, designated to be held on July 30. Detroit Archbishop Allen Vigneron celebrated a Mass at St. Bonaventure Monastery Chapel in front of a full crowd on Sunday, July 29, 2018. Paula Medina Zarate (at far right in the below photograph), whom the Catholic Church declared was cured of a skin disease because of prayers to Father Solanus, visited from Panama for the week of events. (Both, photograph by Jeff Kowalsky.)

This photograph of Blessed Solanus Casey is featured on his prayer cards. The Prayer for Canonization of Fr. Solanus Casey asks that he be declared a saint in the Catholic Church. The prayer is as follows: "O God, I adore You. I give myself to You. May I be the person You want me to be, and may Your will be done in my life today. I thank You for the gifts You gave to Father Solanus. If it is Your will, bless us with the canonization of Father Solanus so that others may imitate and carry on his love for all the poor and suffering of our world. As he joyfully accepted Your divine plans, I ask You, according to Your will, to hear my prayer [your intention] through Jesus Christ our Lord, Amen."

BIBLIOGRAPHY

Baer, Campion R. *Lady Poverty Revisited: A History of the Province of St. Joseph of the Capuchin Order.* Detroit, MI: Lesnau Printing, 2005.

Casey, Bernadine. *God Bless You and Yours: Letters from Solanus Casey, OFM Cap.* Detroit, MI: The Father Solanus Guild, 2000.

Crosby, Michael. *Solanus Casey: The Official Account of a Virtuous American Life.* New York: The Crossroad Publishing Company, 2002.

———. *Thank God Ahead of Time: The Life and Spirituality of Solanus Casey.* Cincinnati, OH: Franciscan Media, 2009.

Derum, James Patrick. *The Porter of Saint Bonaventure's: The Life of Father Solanus Casey, Capuchin.* Detroit, MI: The Fidelity Press, 1968.

Odell, Catherine M. *Father Solanus Casey: Revised and Updated.* Huntington, IN: Our Sunday Visitor Publishing Division, 2017.

Wollenweber, Leo. *Meet Solanus Casey: Spiritual Counselor and Wonder Worker.* Cincinnati, OH: Franciscan Media, 2002.

About the Organization

The impact of Blessed Solanus Casey's ministry lives on today through the Capuchin Order's outreach to the poor and the disadvantaged.

The Solanus Casey Center, which so movingly illustrates the friar's service, is open seven days per week. At the Solanus Casey Center, the life of the Capuchin friar is showcased through the everyday items he touched and cherished—his rosary beads, his violin, and the weathered robe he wore. Guided group tours are available. For more information, visit www.solanuscenter.org.

The Father Solanus Guild was founded in 1960 by laypeople committed to promoting the legacy of this remarkable priest. Its 35,000 members, located in the United States and in at least 23 other countries, promote his cause for canonization and the spirituality exemplified by Father Solanus. The Capuchin friars remember the intentions of members in daily prayer and Masses. Visit www.solanuscasey.org for more information.

The Capuchins' Detroit footprint will grow in the coming years due to the generosity of Art Van Elslander, founder of the Michigan-based Art Van furniture store that became a nationwide chain, who died in February 2018. In December 2017, the longtime Capuchin supporter announced a multimillion-dollar donation to expand the Solanus Casey Center and enhance the surrounding neighborhood. Plans include more green space to allow for outdoor Masses and additional parking, an outdoor votive chapel, and other improvements.

Blessed Solanus Casey helped cofound the Capuchin Soup Kitchen (CSK), which serves more than 2,000 meals daily. The CSK also provides more than a meal. Its programs assist those making transitions out of addiction and imprisonment, and those who may lack education and/or job skills. Donations to aid Capuchin ministries may be mailed to Capuchin Development Office, 1820 Mount Elliott Street, Detroit, Michigan, 48207. For more information, visit thecapuchins.org.

St. Bonaventure Monastery in Detroit, where Father Solanus first entered the Capuchins and where he ministered for many years, welcomes all visitors. A morning Mass is held daily in the chapel where Solanus prayed. At 2:00 p.m. each Wednesday and Sunday, St. Bonaventure holds a "Blessing of the Sick" service and offers individual blessings for those seeking solace to deal with physical and spiritual concerns.

DISCOVER THOUSANDS OF LOCAL HISTORY BOOKS FEATURING MILLIONS OF VINTAGE IMAGES

Arcadia Publishing, the leading local history publisher in the United States, is committed to making history accessible and meaningful through publishing books that celebrate and preserve the heritage of America's people and places.

Find more books like this at
www.arcadiapublishing.com

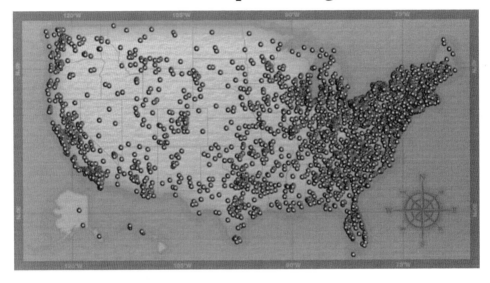

Search for your hometown history, your old stomping grounds, and even your favorite sports team.